This book belongs to:

....

....

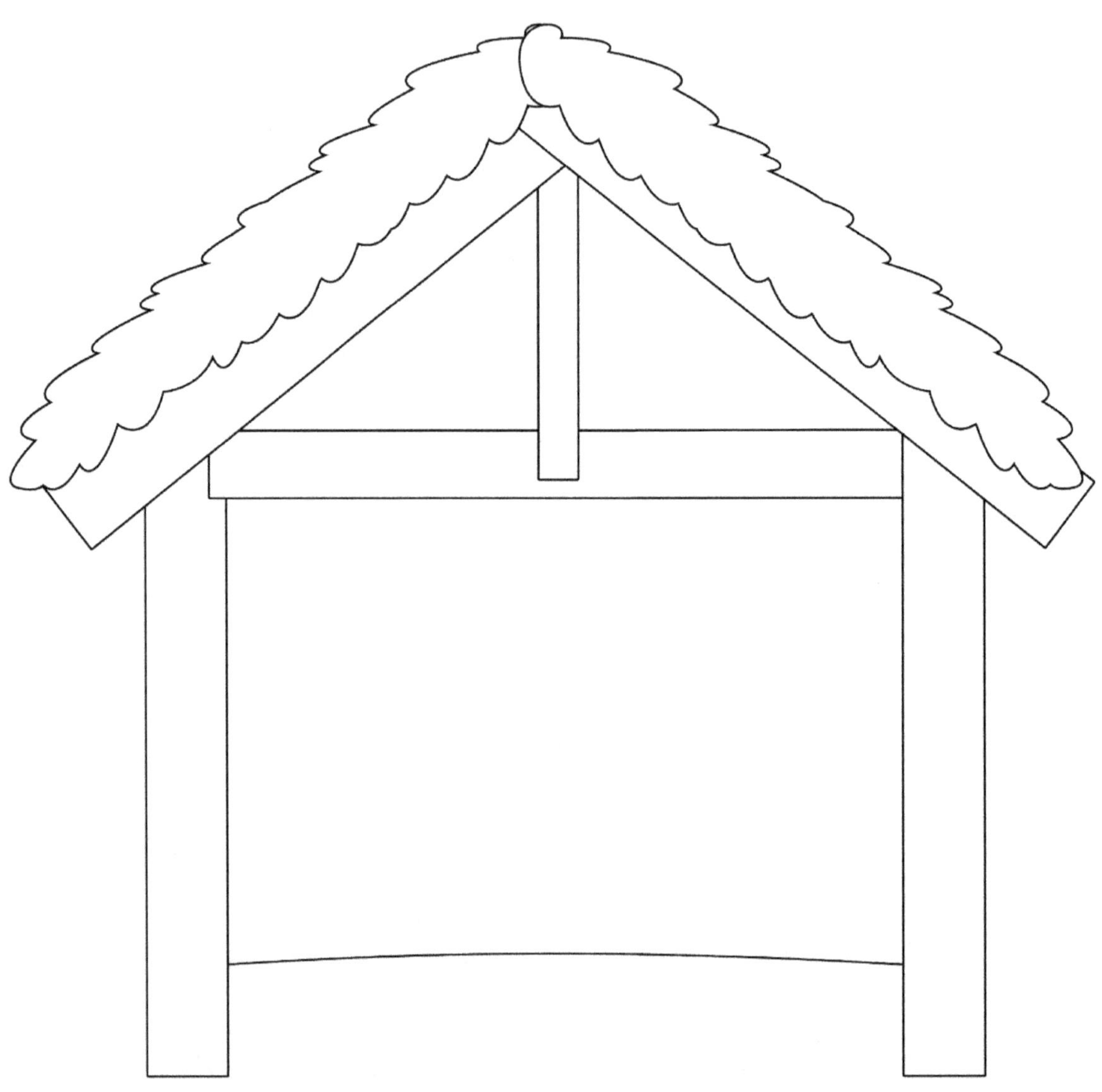

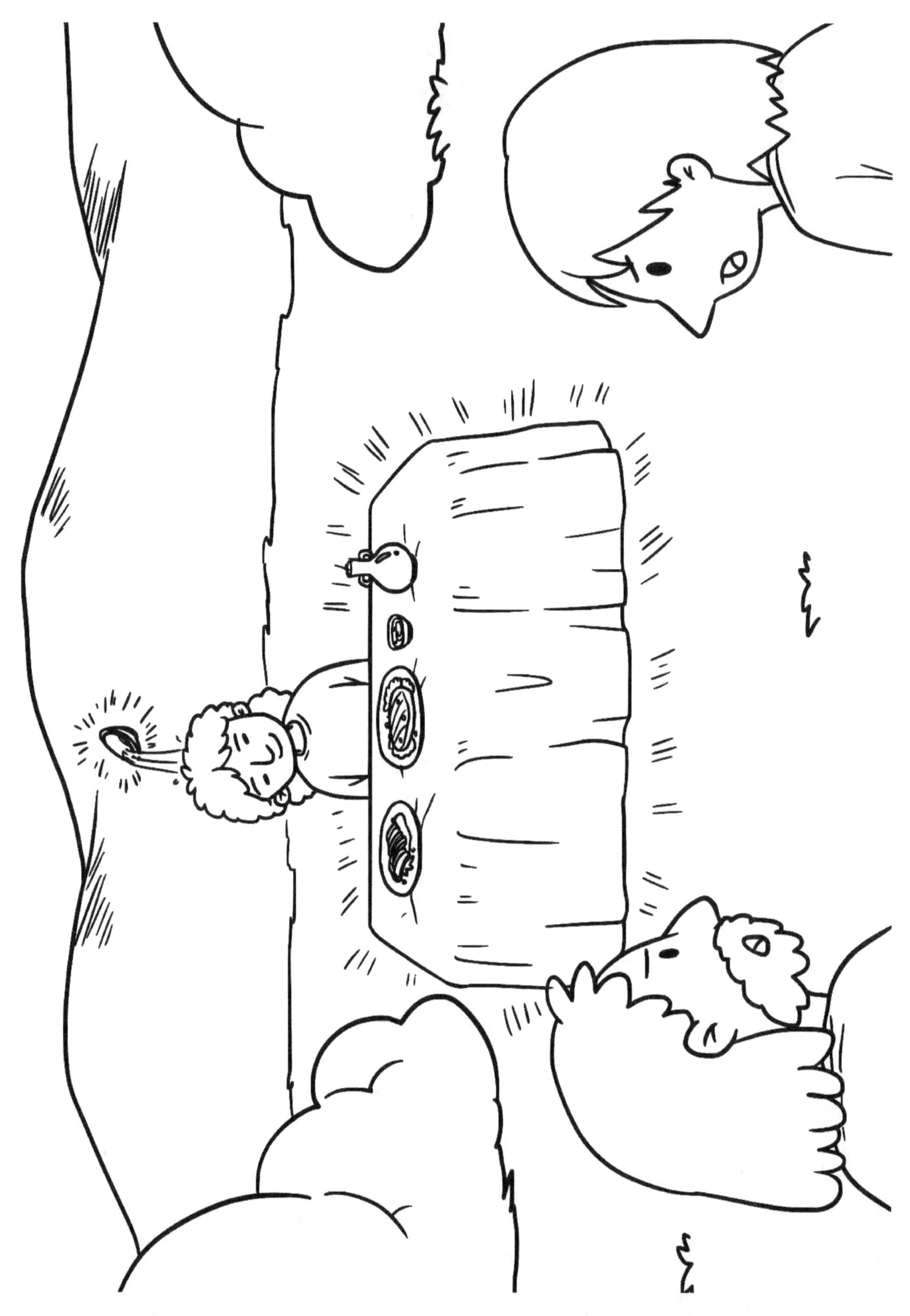

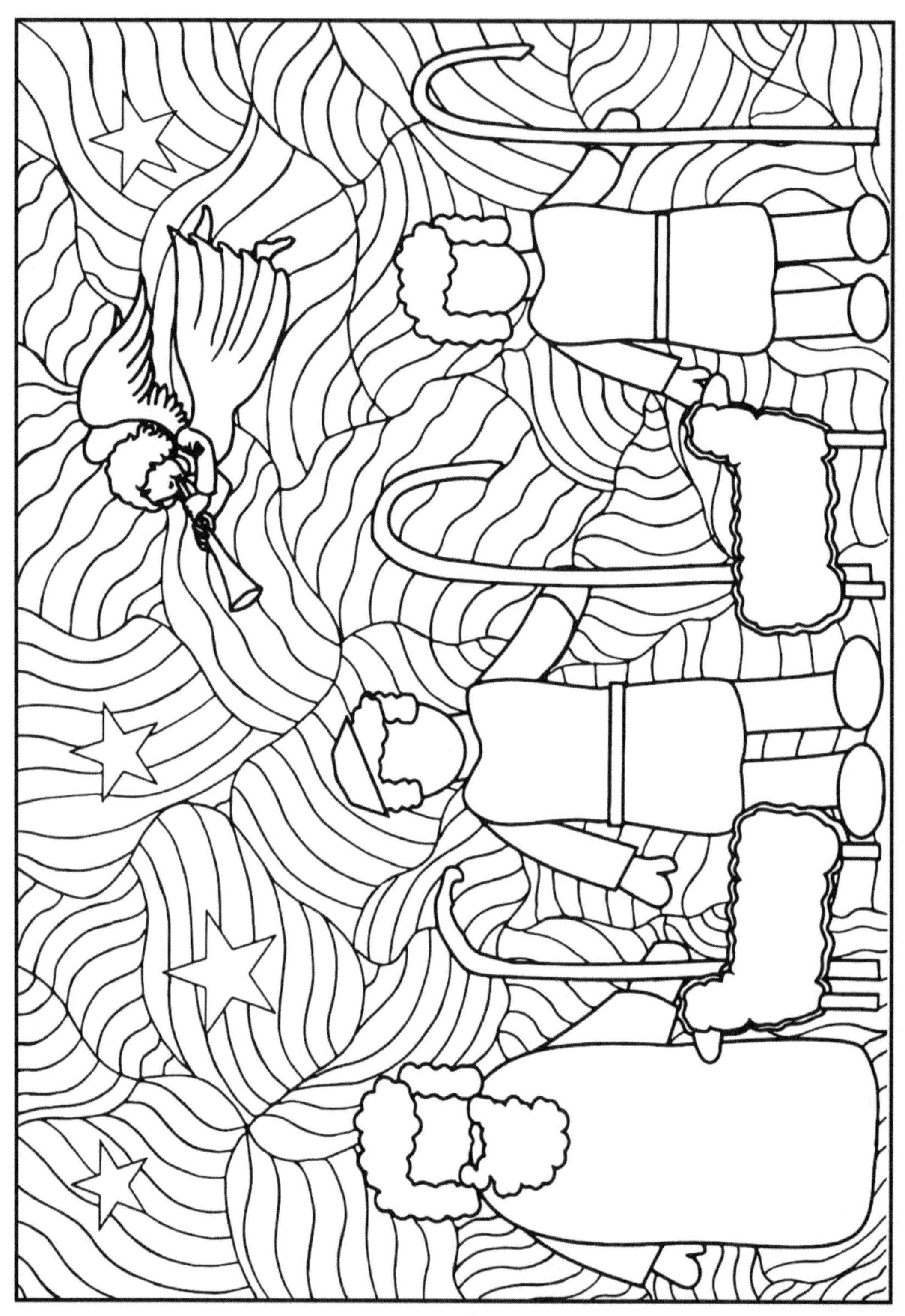

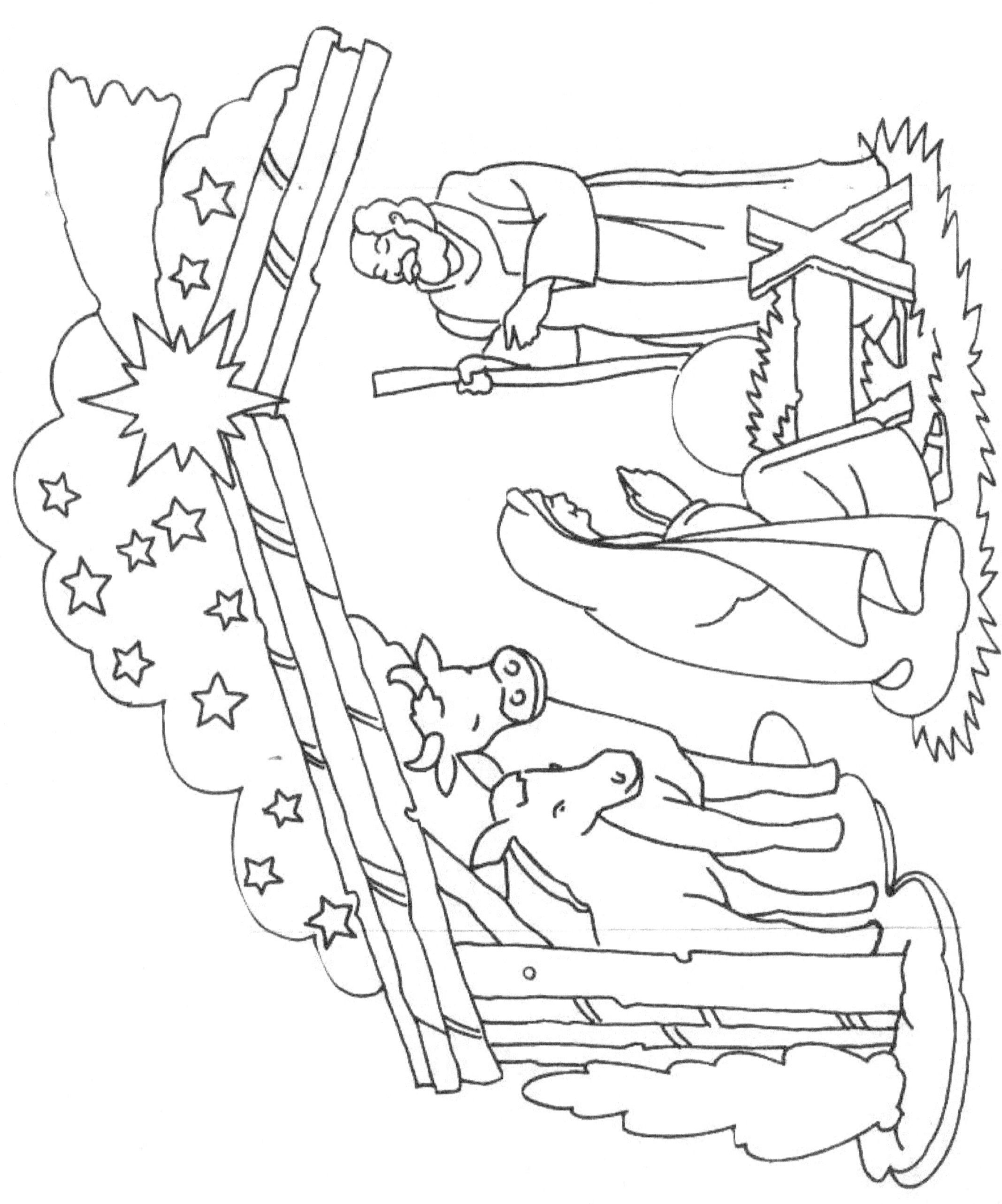

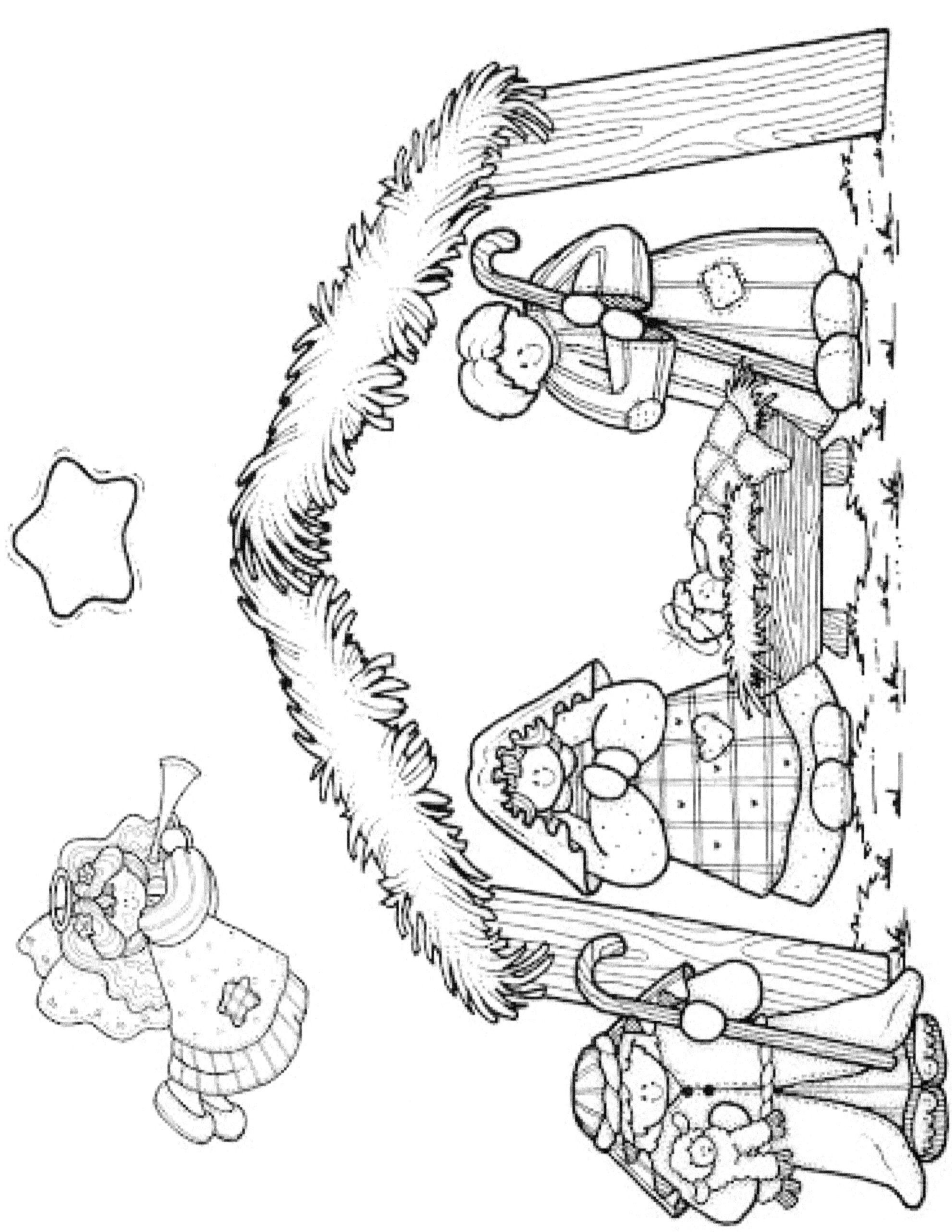

Good News of great Joy
a Savior
Christ the Lord
hope ink

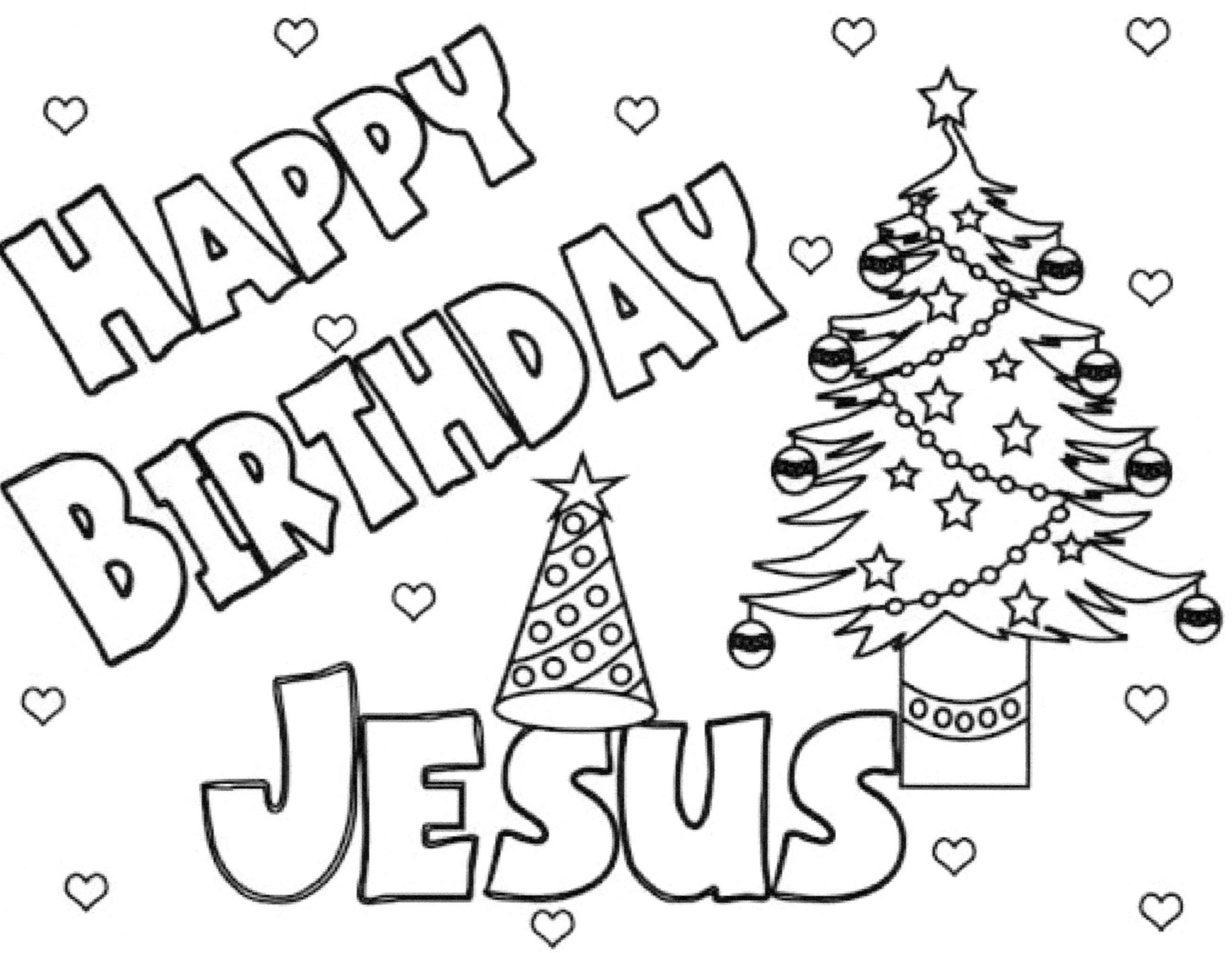

HAPPY
BIRTHDAY
JESUS

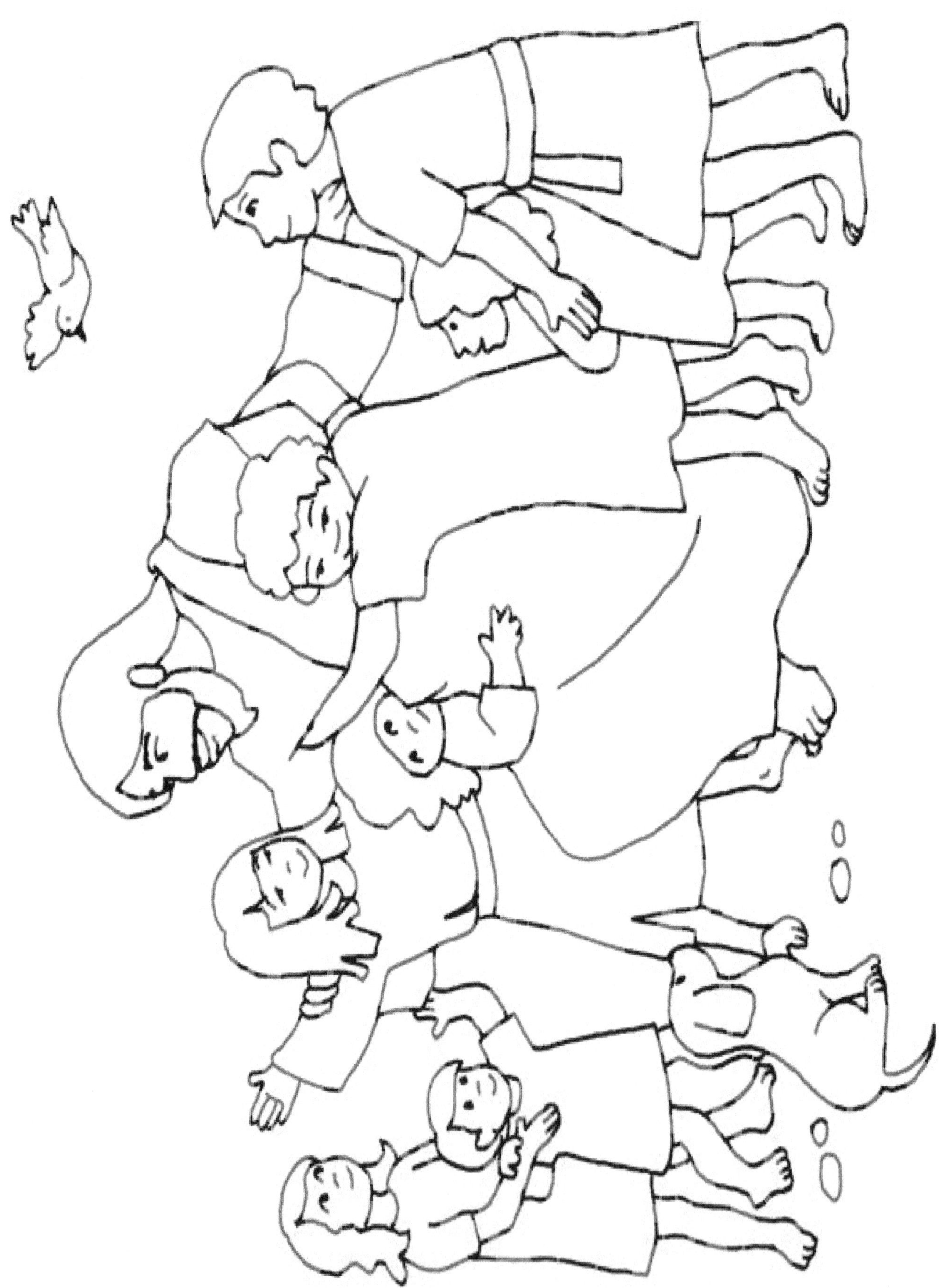